The sale of this book without its cover is unauthorized. If you purchased this book without a cover, you should be aware that it was reported to the publisher as "unsold and destroyed." Neither the authors nor the publisher has received payment for the sale of this "stripped book."

Published by Three Muses Ink.

www.3musesink.com

Mischief and Might: The Monkey King is a work of fiction. Names, characters, places, and incidents either are the product of the author's imagination or are used fictitiously, and any resemblance to actual persons, living or dead, business establishments, events or locales is entirely coincidental. The publisher does not have any control over and does not assume any responsibility for author or third-party websites or their content.

Kari L. Ronning
Mischief and Might: The Monkey King

Mischief and Might: The Monkey King©2016 Kari Ronning

Cover art, images, art, and graphics are by Kari Ronning©2016, Kari Ronning.

Edited by Daniel Wilson (MrProofReading) https://www.fiverr.com/mrproofreading

ALL RIGHTS RESERVED. This book contains material protected under International and Federal Copyright Laws and Treaties. Any unauthorized reprint or use of this material is prohibited. No part of this book may be reproduced or transmitted in any form or by any means, electronic or mechanical, including photocopying, recording, or by any information storage and retrieval system without express written permission from the author / publisher.

For rights information please email: **manager@3musesink.com**

ISBN 10: 1-946181-95-1
ISBN 13: 978-1-946181-95-4

Library of Congress Control Number: 2016944606

Three Muses Ink presents
Storybook series

Nisse of the Great Tree

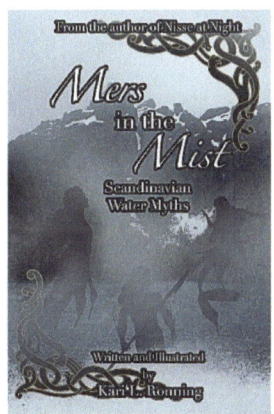

Mers in the Mist: Scandinavian Water Myths

Nisse at Night

www.3MusesInk.com

For my Mother

Mischief and Might: The Monkey King

Written and Illustrated by Kari L. Ronning

www.3MusesInk.com

China has an ancient culture filled with rich magical myth, legend, and story. For centuries, fables about majestic beasts, great tales of heroes and gods, mysterious animals, and wondrous places have delighted children and adults alike, taking them into a world without time, where peaches of immortality can grant longevity, dragons can bless with luck, and creatures from the wood can be filled with wisdom and knowledge. Visit with some of China's most astonishing…

Dragons

Dragons have long been Chinese myths most well-known creatures. Unlike Western stories, they are rarely depicted with wings but are still able to fly with long majestic bodies. Coming in many colors, with gleaming scales, even some fur, dragons have long whiskers, and many shapes of antler-like horns. They are often thought to be very wise with magical control over the elements. They are symbols of great power, strength, and good luck.

LongMu, the Dragon Mother

The myth of LongMu began when she was known as Wen Shi. She found a white stone by the river. Taking it home, she discovered it was an egg that hatched into five baby dragons. She cared for them, even saving them the best food though her family was poor. When the dragons grew, they were able to command the elements. She asked them to summon the rains and ended the drought plaguing her village. She became known as LongMu, mother of dragons. Their story has become a symbol of family and parental love.

Qilin

Qilin, pronounced "chi-lin," are often called the unicorns of Chinese myth. They come in as many colors as there are in the rainbow but are most commonly thought to be gold. Unlike typical unicorns, Qilin have beautiful scales and fur or feathers. They usually have more than one horn, like dragons. Graceful and pure, Qilin's voices sound like bells. They are considered lucky and a vision of prosperity, able to judge the guilty and protect the innocent.

Feng Huang

The Feng Huang, often associated with the Phoenix, is the ruler of Birds, majestic, graceful, and most beautiful. It is extremely kind and embodies the five virtues: benevolence, righteousness, propriety, wisdom, and sincerity.

It never harms an insect or a blade of grass and only drinks sweet spring water and eats bamboo seeds.

Pixiu

A pixiu, pronounced "pa-hsui", is a great winged lion that patrols the sky, keeping away demons, ghosts, and disease.
It is fierce and powerful, capable of driving away evil spirits and leaving happiness and wealth in their place. It is considered a house guardian animal, also called the "fortune beast."

Chinese myth has so many wonderful creatures with stories dating to times before we had dates.

One that remains beloved even today is the mischievous and mighty Monkey King.

The Monkey King's name is Sun Wukong. He also refers to himself as "Great Sage, Equal of Heaven."

He lives on the beautiful Mountain of Flowers and Fruit.

He was born from a magical stone, which transformed one day into a magical stone egg. When wind blew against the egg, out popped Sun Wukong.

He played with the other animals and monkeys on the mountain until, one day, he went through a waterfall all the monkeys were afraid to venture through.
They said, whoever would go through the water would be their king. Unafraid, Sun Wukong went through the water and became the Monkey King.

The Monkey King is very powerful. He can lift heavy objects with ease. He is even stronger than many of the mighty warriors in the Heavenly Courts of the Gods.

He can jump over 13,000 miles in one summersault, even over a mountain.

The Monkey King can transform himself into 72 different things, like animals, weapons, plants, and objects.

Though he can hide well when he transforms, he has a hard time completely transforming his tail. It tends to give him away. A monkey's tail is very important.

The hair of the Monkey King is especially magical. Each hair can make copies of himself or other transformations. He was once attacked by 1,000 swords, so he took a few hairs and created 1,000 shields that broke the swords.

The Monkey King can also do spells. One can command the air; another will part the waters. He can create protective circles and even freeze someone in place.

His magical staff is named Ruyi Jingu Bang. He won it from the Dragon King of the Eastern Sea. The great weapon is a golden-banded staff that weighs 8.1 tons. The staff's true master is the Monkey King, and it glows to acknowledge him.

The staff is able to shrink and grow and even fight as directed without the Monkey King holding it. When he is not using it, he shrinks it down to the size of needle and keeps it tucked behind his ear.

The Monkey King had many adventures, battling armies of the gods and causing much havoc in heaven with his mischief. The gods tried to control him by trying to trick him or imprison him, but the Monkey King was far too clever and skilled.

He even stole some of the Sacred Peaches of Immorality from the Empress Mother's garden. Immortal, as one of the gods now, the Monkey King continues to defy heaven's rules.

His playfulness and might echoes in the hearts of readers, continuing to make Sun Wukong one of China's most beloved and fabled characters.

Kari L. Ronning
Author and Artist

Kari is the principle artist and author of the publishing company, Three Muses Ink. She is a full time artist and writer with a Bachelor's of Art from the University of Alaska. Kari is an award-winning photographer who specializes in digital composites, digital and traditional drawing and painting, and graphic design.

Passionate about writing and storytelling, she's been a spinner of tales and an imaginative illustrator since grade school. A long-standing love of elves, myth, and legends influenced by her Norwegian and Chinese heritage, sparked a talent in creating fantasy themed novels, art and narratives. Across multiple genres, the interests have come together in works such as the Haunted Weir Workings series, Nisse at Night, a fully illustrated Norwegian themed children's story, and many other projects from Three Muses Ink.

Three Muses Ink

Three Muses Ink is a trio of authors and artists from the great northern state of Alaska. Always fans of fantasy and storytelling, the love affair with the idea of creating our own world started early. We are inseparable friends who have turned our passion into an independent publishing company, Three Muses Ink, producing novels, storybooks, artwork, and all manner of artistic creations.

To find out more about Three Muses Ink projects check out our website:
www.3MusesInk.com

www.ingramcontent.com/pod-product-compliance
Lightning Source LLC
Chambersburg PA
CBHW041815040426
42451CB00001B/7